Gift of
James H. Russell

In Memoriam.

MELANCTHON W. JACOBUS,
D.D., LL. D.

Born, September 19, 1816.
Died, October 28, 1876.

Rev. Dr. Melancthon W. Jacobus was suddenly called away from earth, on the morning of Saturday, October 28th, 1876. His accustomed occupations were prosecuted without abatement to the last. But two days before his death he was in consultation with Rev. Dr. C. C. Beatty, the President of the Board of Directors of the Western Theological Seminary, and its most munificent benefactor; busied with plans for the welfare of that institution, and particularly for the alteration and enlargement of one of its principal edifices. It was scarcely two months since the opening of the session, at which he delivered the introductory lecture; returning with fresh zeal and apparently invigorated health to his work, from which the offer of the Secretaryship of the Board of Education had failed to draw him. His reasons for declining that position, which had been urgently pressed upon him, will appear from a brief extract from a letter written at the time:—

"You may be surprised to learn that, after weighing all my duty in regard to the Secretaryship, I am not able to see my way clear to accept the invitation. The work would take me so entirely off my track of life-long occupation, — in the office and on the wing, vindicating the cause, and appealing for funds, and taking a sort of oversight of candidates, — that I find myself shrinking from it, and fearing that my nervous system might not bear the strain. I therefore more readily fall in with the protests from Allegheny, and with the counsel of many Eastern friends, who say that, while I am the man for the post, it is doubtful whether it is the post for me. And, much as I should like the idea of rendering the church important service, I cannot be sure that even at self-sacrifice I should be able to endure it. I wait, then, the will and providence of God. I would like to pursue my Biblical studies, and put my material of twenty-five years into shape. Perhaps I may have mistaken my duty; but I have every way sought light."

The Synod of Pittsburgh, of which he was a member, being in session but a few days before he died, he was present, and took an active part in its proceedings. He addressed the Synod upon various matters which were under discussion, and particularly made an earnest appeal on behalf of the cause of sustentation, in which he continued to take a lively interest; having been from the first profoundly convinced of its vast, and even vital, importance to the Presbyterian Church; having demonstrated its feasibility practically by setting it in operation and for four years conducting its affairs as its Secretary, without salary, and, in a manner that commanded the confidence of the church, received the unqualified commendation of its highest judicatory, and vindicated for it a place among the permanent schemes of the church; and still cherishing an unwavering confidence in its ultimate success, notwithstanding the apathy of some and the discouragement of others.

On the day before his death, he lectured in the Seminary, as usual, and with his accustomed vivacity and vigor. The next morning, the community was startled with the intelligence that he was no more.

The funeral solemnities were conducted partly at Pittsburgh, and partly at Newark, N. J., his ancestral home, to which his remains were conveyed for interment. After prayer by Rev. Prof. Samuel T. Lowrie, D.D., at the house in Allegheny, where Dr. JACOBUS had so long resided, the sad procession moved to the First Presbyterian Church in Pittsburgh, which was thronged in every part by a deeply sympathizing audience. Prayer was offered by Rev. Dr. S. F. Scovel and Dr. A. A. Hodge. Appropriate passages of Scripture were read by Rev. Dr. S. J. Niccols, and addresses were made by Rev. Dr. Hornblower and Dr. C. C. Beatty. When these services were ended, the bereaved family took the train for the East, accompanied by representatives of the professors, directors, trustees, and students of the Western Theological Seminary, and by a delegation from the Cliosophic Society of the College of New Jersey. At the appointed hour, the friends assembled at the house of Mrs. George A. Keen, in Newark, where prayer was offered by Rev. Dr. Craven; who also conducted the devotional exercises in the church, aided by Rev. Dr. McCosh, and Rev. John Hall, D.D., of New York City. Addresses were made by Rev. William M. Paxton, D.D., Rev. Prof. Samuel J. Wilson, D.D., and Rev. William Adams, D.D.

The several addresses that were delivered here follow, in their order; and to these are appended a few extracts from some of the numerous letters received from friends, and some tributes to the memory of Dr. JACOBUS by different associations.

SERVICES

IN

THE FIRST PRESBYTERIAN CHURCH,

PITTSBURGH, PA.

ADDRESS OF THE REV. W. H. HORNBLOWER, D.D.

"Know ye not that there is a prince and a great man fallen this day in Israel?" — 2 SAM. iii. 38.

THE duty of addressing you to-day has been devolved upon me, for the simple reason that my acquaintance with him we mourn, and would honor, began in early boyhood, and extends over the entire period of his active life. Our parents were members of the same church; our fathers were both elders of that church; and we were both baptized by the hands of the same pastor, the Rev. James Richards, D.D., afterwards Professor in the Theological Seminary at Auburn, N. Y.

My review of the first part of his life is greatly aided by an autobiography which he had recently begun.

MELANCTHON WILLIAMS JACOBUS, born in Newark, N. J., Sept. 19th, 1816, was the son of godly parents, Peter and Phebe Williams Jacobus, who consecrated him in his infancy to the holy ministry. He was the eldest of six children. The character of his parents may be judged by the fact, that one of his sisters, Elizabeth, died at five years of age, "giving marvellous evidence of the Christian life," as he writes in his manuscript. I remember hearing much of this remarkable child, and reading a brief memoir of her life that was published at the time of her death.

This oldest child, consecrated to the ministry by his pious parents, was as precocious in intellect as his younger sister was in piety. At eight years of age he was studying Latin and Greek, at the then famous "Newark Academy," taught by Abraham Van Doren, Principal, and his talented sons, J. Livingston, Luther Halsey, and J. Howard Van Doren, Assistants. Five years later, when the Newark Academy had passed into less able hands, I became a pupil of the same institution, and have a very vivid recollection of MELANCTHON JACOBUS. Though only thirteen years of age, his associates in his classes were much older than himself, — some of them no longer boys, but young men. He seemed to me, therefore, "one of the big boys"; and this made the kind attentions he bestowed upon me appear as a graceful condescension on his part, and an honor on mine. A bright, high-spirited, quick-tempered boy, wild and mischievous, he was regarded by the whole school as a leader whom it was chivalric to imitate and follow. He was not the standard model of a " good boy." Notwithstanding the pious efforts of his parents, and the attendance on weekly prayer-meetings, and the exercise of taking notes of the sermons on Sunday morning, and of repeating the texts and divisions to his father, and of writing out as much of the sermon as he could recollect on Sunday evenings, — all of which had a very beneficial effect on him, — his too intimate association with the large number of workmen in his father's employ was a damaging influence; and, as he himself writes, but " for the grace of God," might have wrought his ruin.

At the age of fourteen he was sent to school at the Academy in Bloomfield, N. J. His father was induced to send him there, he says, because at that very time there was a revival of religion in the church of Bloomfield, and in this particular school, taught by Rev. Albert Pierson. Among his associates in this school, he mentions the names of three candidates for the ministry, who afterwards became distinguished for usefulness, — Peter Dougherty, one of the first missionaries of our Presbyterian Board to the Indians, and who accomplished a work among some bands of the Chippewas and Ottawas, on the Grand and Little Traverse Bays, in the State of Michigan, excelled by nothing in the annals of missionary labor among American Indians; John H. Morrison, who to-day is the oldest American missionary, still active and useful, in India; and Elias J. Richards, a man of rare endowments, a successful pastor, in Paterson, N. J., in the city of Philadelphia, and in Reading, Pa., where he continued many years, and ended a useful life six years ago. These earnest men produced a profound impression on the character of young JACOBUS. But their influence, and that of others who sought to win him for Christ, was counteracted by that of a physician with whom he boarded, and who dissuaded him from attending the revival meetings. But he could not resist the power of God's Spirit. A strong conviction, that "godliness is profitable for this world as well as for the world to come," led him to resolve to seek the great salvation. Manfully he confessed his purpose to his medical friend, who replied, "If you go to the meetings, I will go with you." The result was the conversion of both of them.

In the Seminary chapel, about a year ago, Dr. JACOBUS related his experience in this happy change of his life. Those who heard him will recall it in the less full and animated account contained in his manuscript: "I strove to find peace; to get a hope, as it was called. I heard of *frames* and processes through which others had passed, — tears, darkness, deep convictions of sin, followed by sudden light. I could get no such coveted exercises. I fell upon my knees in my chamber, read Nettleton's Village Hymns and the Bible, if possibly the conviction and tears and agony might come as with others. But *no!* The more I labored for such a hope, the more impossible it was to me, till at length I said to myself, 'If I cannot be saved without passing through such processes, I cannot be saved at all,' when the thought flashed across me, 'Thou fool! looking for your spectacles when they are on your nose. Jesus has wept and agonized and died for me, and all this preparation and provision is completed for me by Him!' Here I rested in Christ and His finished work. Oh, blessed thought!"

At this time the great and apostolical Dr. Nettleton was holding meetings in Newark. It was at one of these meetings that I again met my old school friend. We were seated in the same pew, in the gallery of the old First Church, and after the meeting he addressed me very faithfully and affectionately about my soul. He made several efforts afterwards to bring me to Christ; and, though they were not successful efforts, they left a deep impression on my heart, and I ever after entertained for him a peculiar regard. He was the first one, near my own age, who ever seemed to care for my soul.

Previous to his conversion, he had intended to study law. But "now his purpose was suddenly and positively changed." There was no "attraction to him for the ministry," he says, "in a secular and a social point of view." But the divine call could not be resisted. When only fourteen years of age, he was received into the full communion of the First Church of Newark. On account of his youth, the Session hesitated to admit him, and held his application under consideration for three months before they granted his request.

In the month of September, 1831, when still lacking a few days of his fifteenth year, he entered the Sophomore Class of Princeton College. Though the youngest member of his class, he carried off its highest honors in each successive year. He, with Parke Godwin, — now known as editor of the "New York Post" and a writer of History, — and the now sainted Elias J. Richards, were representatives of the Cliosophic Society, among the junior orators of his class. At his graduation, he shared the first honor with Edward Pendleton, of Martinsburgh, W. Va. At that time it was the custom in Princeton College to bestow certain honors, distinguished as first, second, &c., and each honor was often divided among a number of competitors. To take the *first honor solus* was regarded as a great distinction. In the case of Mr. JACOBUS, although Mr. Pendleton shared the honor with him, yet, on account of his youth and other circumstances, it was judged that his merit was equal to that of taking the first honor *solus;* and the Cliosophic Society conferred upon him a mark of appreciation to which this distinction would have entitled him. At the time of his graduation, when not quite eighteen years of age, the Trustees of Princeton College elected him a tutor. He was pressed to accept the position; but, by the advice of Dr. James Richards, determined to lose no time in preparing himself for the gospel ministry.

After his graduation from college, he spent a year in his father's office. Here he developed such extraordinary business talent that his best friends urged him to relinquish his intentions of studying for the ministry, and devote himself to mercantile pursuits. Even his pious father, who had consecrated him to the ministry, impressed by his genius for business, urged upon him a partnership in his own prosperous manufactory. "Yet," he says, "I was never for a moment moved even to doubt about my great high-calling to the ministry."

In the fall of 1835, he entered the Theological Seminary at Princeton, N. J. His course here was as successful as it had been in the college. Among his associates were men who have risen to the highest distinction in the church. He was one of a private class instructed by Dr. J. Addison Alexander "in special Hebrew studies." "This elegant scholar," he says, referring to Dr. J. Addison Alexander, "took a lively interest in me, and gave into my hands the Book of Malachi, to prepare a commentary, which I did, in my way. This exercise seemed to direct my studies in the department of exegesis, and thus a taste was developed for this kind of investigation."

At the end of his seminary course, he was invited to remain as "tutor in Hebrew, and assistant of Dr. J. Addison Alexander." This offer was accepted.

He became, at this time, an intimate friend of the

celebrated Hebraist, Dr. Isaac Nordheimer, who inducted him into the study of Arabic and Syriac. Dr. Nordheimer enlisted him as an assistant in several linguistic projects he had in view, but which he did not live to complete.

His career in the Seminary covered the period of the greatest convulsion in our Presbyterian Church, which issued in the division of the Church into two parties, — the New and the Old School. Here the firmness of his own convictions was again tried. All his friends in Newark were "strongly in sympathy with the party which was led by Dr. Fisher and Dr. Richards. But my own mind," he says, "was fixed on the side of the standards and the true succession, as I understood it." Though he dismisses the whole subject, in his manuscript, in the single sentence I have quoted, I have no doubt he suffered more, and displayed more heroism, in adhering to his convictions than he chose, in these days of a reunited church, to record.

In the year of his tutorship, 1839, he was licensed to preach the gospel by the Presbytery of New Brunswick. At that time, the students of Princeton were not permitted to receive license till arrived at the end of the three years' course in the Seminary. Neither were they suffered to exercise their gifts in preaching, except in the class-room, or in the way of addresses and speeches at prayer-meetings and Sunday-schools. Dr. JACOBUS complains of this, and feelingly describes the hardship of being suddenly thrust into the pulpit, without any previous experience in the delivery of sermons to a promiscuous congregation.

Towards the close of the year 1839, he was, most unexpectedly to himself, called to the pastorship of the First Presbyterian Church in Brooklyn, N. Y. Here his own manuscript ends. Two or three pages before this ending is this sadly interesting note: "September 19, 1876. This day — a brilliant sky and invigorating air — I am sixty years old, writing these reminiscences of early life, thankful to a covenant God for His great goodness, wherewith He has distinguished my lot, and *hopeful for other years of usefulness.*"

Alas! that hopefulness for other "years of usefulness" was not to be realized. It is pleasant to know that he was not depressed and haunted with painful dread of the impending event; that he had no gloomy forebodings of the fact that, instead of "*years,*" only *five weeks* remained for "usefulness" on earth. And yet how sad for us, that a life so full of spirit and energy was to be so soon and suddenly terminated; the pen of the ready writer, to fall from the skilful hand; and the "reminiscences," begun with such lively interest, to perish for ever beyond the power of human recovery!

What remains of the public life of Dr. JACOBUS has already been written and published. We need not recapitulate the details. In the church, in its controversies, in its benevolent enterprises, in its ecclesiastical courts, he has been an active participant. He has attained the highest ecclesiastical honors that could be conferred upon him. The scholastic degrees of D.D. and LL.D. adorn his name. He is associated, historically, with the grandest event in the history of our church, — as Moderator of the Old School Assembly at the time of the reunion; at the meetings of the General Assembly in 1869, in May at New York, and in November at Pittsburgh; in the union meeting of both Assemblies in the Third Church of Pittsburgh; and as Moderator at the opening of the reunited Assembly in Philadelphia, May, 1870. The dignity, the wisdom, the piety, he displayed at this period were universally admired; and the speeches he delivered and the public prayers he offered, in his official character as Moderator, were of such superlative excellence that many, and among them some who were not carried away with the enthusiastic fever for reunion, were disposed to regard him as inspired by the Holy Spirit of God. His published writings, emphatically his commentaries, have extended his fame to Europe, and will communicate it to ages to come. All these facts have passed into history.

But you who are assembled here to-day are mourning for him as a genial friend, a popular preacher, and, to some of you, in former years a dearly beloved pastor. The versatility of his mind never appeared to better advantage than in the pulpit and at the prayer-meeting, or on occasions that called for impromptu speech. His extraordinary tact enabled him to adapt himself to all circumstances; and the rapidity of his mental action seized on every passing incident, and derived advantage from the unexpected events and surroundings that would have embarrassed an ordinary man. He was *semper paratus*. One unfailing resource with him in all emergencies was his thorough knowledge of the English Bible. This prince among scholars and ecclesiastics rose above all his peers in other departments of learning, by his familiar acquaintance with the Word of God. The facility and aptness of his Scripture quotations were as surprising as they were edifying. Who can forget the rich and beautiful recitations of Bible sentences beside the sick-bed and at the burial of the dead? How we miss his voice and his Scripture citations to-day! "Would," exclaimed one who spoke what many have thought, — "would that what he uttered at Dr. Howard's funeral was written down, that it might be repeated word for word at his own!"

Another source of his appropriateness in his addresses and speeches was his quick sympathy with others. He took their measure, entered into their minds, and felt with them as well as for them. In his sermons he bridged over the distance between the pulpit and the pews, and lost his own personality in the aggregate mass of the congregation, speaking to them as if he himself were one of them; so that sometimes his sermons and addresses had much of the effect of a colloquy between himself and the people. He would anticipate objections that they might make, or questions they might ask, and put them into words for them; or he would ask them questions, and answer in their place. Sometimes a succession of questions would follow each other, each one answered with his quick, emphatic "yes" or "no," without once allowing his voice to descend into the falling inflection, so that his discourse was like an animated and continuous conversation. Another evidence of his practical knowledge of men, and of his habit of preaching to the average man, was the exhibition of the same truth over and over again, in a great variety of aspects. Sometimes he never got beyond the first simple proposition or idea with which his sermon began. It was presented in different lights and colors and relations; his fancy playing about it, producing often sudden and surprising kaleidoscopic effects, or the subject passing through a succession of dissolving views. The rhetorician might regard this as a homiletical fault; but, in the man who addresses the people, it is an invaluable element of success, such as William Pitt and Thomas Chalmers studied to effect. Dr. JACOBUS preached a sermon in this pulpit, one evening, of which a critic truthfully remarked, "There was nothing in the whole sermon that was not substantially contained in the first five minutes of its delivery." The next evening, at the young men's prayer-meeting in the room behind this pulpit, all the remarks and prayers were tinctured, colored, permeated, with the sermon of the previous evening. Those who spoke and prayed did not appear conscious of the fact; at least, there was not a single direct allusion made to the sermon or the preacher. But the one thought of that sermon had got into their thoughts and hearts, without their knowing it. Dr. JACOBUS understood that, in preaching to the average man, it is not enough to present a truth clearly and prove it incontestably, but that it must be driven home into the man's soul by reiterated blows of the rhetorical hammer.

The adaptation of his ordinary sermons and addresses to the people consisted, again, in avoiding a severely logical structure or a brilliant display of imaginative power. His logic, discarding artificial forms, was addressed to the common sense, the ordinary judgments, of men; and his motives, to the affections, principles, and passions that characterize our human nature. In some of his earlier sermons, the creative faculty was largely employed. I remember one, preached in the First Church of Newark, on the Foundation Stones of the New Jerusalem, in which there was much novelty, and some fine flights of imagination. He has told me that, at that period of his life, he often sought out new paths, and aimed at originality and striking effects.

But the wise counsels of that great man, Dr. James W. Alexander, who regarded him in his youth with affectionate interest, led him to correct this tendency, and regard chiefly the practical results of preaching, — to aim at benefiting rather than pleasing his hearers. But though he preached old truths, and made practical applications, he always employed new materials to render them fresh and vigorous; and so illuminated them by the play of his fancy that no hearer, of whatever degree of intellectuality or culture, could fail to be interested and instructed. He was, indeed, a "scribe instructed unto the kingdom of heaven, like unto a man that is an householder, which bringeth forth out of his treasure things new and old." — MATT. xiii. 52.

There have been more eloquent preachers, — preachers with larger and higher gifts of oratory; but never was Dr. JACOBUS excelled as a successful preacher to those classes of intellectual and business men who constitute the mass of our Presbyterian Church. And, in debate and discussion in ecclesiastical assemblies, the fertility of his mind, the vehemence of his feelings, and the rapidity with which he caught ideas and grasped conclusions, gave him extraordinary effectiveness.

How can we speak as we ought of Dr. JACOBUS in his connection with the Western Theological Seminary? We must leave it to others to tell how much that institution owes to him; and we must leave it to the students who have graduated there to tell what his personal power on the ministers of the church and of the age has effected. Our grief at his loss is intensified, because we had just, as it were, received him back again to the chair that he had almost vacated, and, with hopes of increased usefulness, concentrating all his abilities in his professorial work, and resuming it with apparently re-established health and a new fervor of enthusiasm and spiritual consecration. I doubt if ever the Faculty entered on a new session with greater satisfaction or higher hopes: each member of it in health, and the others strengthened by the assurance that our senior Professor — our head and chief, our prince — could not be charmed away from us.

As the genial friend, Dr. JACOBUS was loved by many. In the more intimate and sacred relations of his household, we have only to say to those who could not judge for themselves, that it would be impossible to exaggerate the tenderness of his love, the sweetness of his temper, the cheerfulness of his disposition, and the unselfishness of his consideration for others. His home was bright with sunshine, and all who entered it were irradiated with its happiness.

This prince among men, among scholars, and among divines, has ascended into the higher glory, to receive a new diadem. Without pain, — or more than slight sensations of faintness and exhaustion, — in an instant he passed away from earth, working to the last moment: at Synod last week, one of the most active members, speaking often and with all his usual animation; in his class-rooms last week, never more interested and instructive than during the last hour he spent with the Junior Class on Friday morning; no time lost by prolonged sickness, he was translated in an instant from work to rest, and is not, for God hath taken him.

When we lose our friends, our memories linger tenderly about the last events of their lives; and in these, often, we find evidences of a special Providence, shaping and preparing things for the approaching end, that neither they nor we had apprehended. So is it in the case of Dr. JACOBUS.

The opening address of the present term of the Western Theological Seminary was delivered by him. His theme,—"Bible Study: Professional and Popular." The substance of this address was afterwards published, in four successive articles, in the "Presbyterian Banner."

At the last Saturday prayer-meeting and conference before his death, in the Seminary Chapel, Dr. JACOBUS presided, and addressed the students with unusual animation.[1]

The last sermon he preached was delivered in the Second Church of Steubenville, Ohio, Oct. 8th, 1876, on the text, Acts x. 38: "Who went about doing good."[2] The last sermon heard by the members of his own family was delivered in Dr. Swift's pulpit, First Church of Allegheny, Aug. 13th, 1876. The text was Hebrews vii. 25: "Wherefore He is able also to save them to the uttermost that come unto God by Him, seeing He ever liveth to make intercession for them." In the

---

[1] This meeting was a fortnight before the Saturday of his death. On the intervening Saturday, the meeting was omitted on account of the absence of the professors at Synods.

[2] The last sermon preached to his former pastoral charge, the Central Church of Pittsburgh, was on the significant text, "Your Fathers, where are they? and the Prophets, do they live for ever?"—ZECH. i. 5.

manuscript the words "*to the uttermost*" are emphasized by having the original Greek words written above them,— εἰς τὸ παντελές. The last head of the sermon is, "Jesus is able to save *to the uttermost limit of this mortal existence.*" And the last words are a description of the Christian's experience in the final moment of life: "At that uttermost extremity, when all earthly helpers must give up and can do no further work of relief or of salvation, Jesus goes on to save,— triumphs there as the only Saviour, displays His supreme and matchless ability to save through and through. Where Death and the Grave defy any and all others, see how HE saves to the very completion, saves from the bitterness and sting of death, saves even from the *fear* of death, saves from impatience and repining amidst the dying agonies, saves from all those overwhelming anxieties that you would think must make the death-bed of a fond parent so terrible! . . . And then you see the salvation in the triumphant calm and peace wrought out for the departing spirit. And victory sits upon the brow, and a longing, longing for the heavenly home seems to throw the fondest earthly home into the shade. And the heavenly society, the kindred and friends who are there, seem so ineffably attractive as to make those dear ones that were most doted on here only secondary and inferior in their charms. And all this is the proof, the shining proof, that Jesus is able to save to the uttermost. And the secret of all this is, that yonder in heaven, at the Father's side, He is busy in His intercessions, — the living Saviour, actively officiating for His dying children, where the dying Stephen saw Him, — praying that they may be with Him where He is, that they may behold His glory! And so He comes down and meets them in the dark valley, with His shepherd's rod and staff; and stands at the dying bed, vanquishing Satan and hushing his malicious accusations, and whispering, Peace! And His own Spirit, the blessed Third Person of the Trinity, is making responsive intercessions in the heart, with groanings that cannot be uttered; taking of the things of Christ, and showing them to the inward sight, while the natural eye is sealing up in death, — opening the vision to celestial glories at the very moment that it is utterly closed to earth.

" 'Trembling, hoping, lingering, flying,
Oh, the *pain*, the BLISS of dying!' "

" 'Oh! had we learned what death alone brings nigh,
The dread had been to live, and not to die.' "

The last texts of Scripture that connect themselves with him who was so full of texts, and so quick and wonderfully apt in their citation, were precisely those he himself might have chosen. "The Silent Comforter," a roll containing texts for every day, and indicating chapters for daily reading, hangs in his study, and bears the marks of constant use. It was found open for the twenty-eighth day of the month, — the day of his translation. Probably he himself the night before had turned the leaf, that his eye might rest on the right page in the morning. It was at least a pleasant coincidence that the texts his eye last rested on and the Scriptures for that day's reading were these: —

Job xix. 25-27: "For I know that my Redeemer liveth, and that He shall stand at the latter day upon the earth: and though after my skin worms destroy this body, yet in my flesh shall I see God: whom I shall see for myself, and mine eyes shall behold, and not another; though my reins be consumed within me."

Psalm xvii. 15: "As for me, I will behold Thy face in righteousness: I shall be satisfied when I awake with Thy likeness."

The Scripture lessons were Psalm xvi. and 1 Thessalonians iv. The last subject I happened to hear him discussing, in conversation with his associate professor, Dr. Lowrie, was the Messianic character of this sixteenth Psalm. In that Psalm occur the words, "The lines are fallen unto me in pleasant places; yea, I have a goodly heritage;" and the last words are, "Thou wilt show me the path of life: in Thy presence is fulness of joy; at Thy right hand there are pleasures for evermore." The fourth chapter of 1 Thessalonians ends with these glorious words, that have already been read to you: "But I would not have you to be ignorant, brethren, concerning them that are asleep, that ye sorrow not, even as others which have no hope. For if we believe that Jesus died and rose again, even so them also which sleep in Jesus will God bring with Him. For this we say unto you by the word of the Lord, that we which are alive and remain unto the coming of the Lord shall not prevent them which are asleep. For the Lord Himself shall descend from heaven with a shout, with the voice of the archangel, and with the trump of God: and the dead in Christ shall rise first: then we which are alive and remain shall be caught up together with them in the clouds, to meet the Lord in the air: and so shall we ever be with the Lord. Wherefore *comfort one another with these words."*

The last evening of his life was partly occupied in writing to those he loved. There were found lying upon his desk, the next day, sealed, stamped, and addressed, — a letter to his well-beloved physician, a letter to his second daughter, and a postal card to his younger son. In these two last, after speaking, in his playful, punning fashion, of a toothache from which he was suffering, he used these remarkable words: "I hope, providentially, to be relieved on the morrow." It is singular that he should have introduced that word "providentially." Doubtless it gave point to the humor of the moment. Yet we may almost believe that it was dictated by some hidden inner consciousness, unrecognized by himself, but dimly affected by the shadow of that absolute and eternal relief from all pain that was silently approaching.

The very last utterance that passed his lips, the last word to which he gave audible voice, was the name of her who was dearest to him of all on earth, — that wife whose form suggests the image of the fragile reed that bends before a zephyr's breath, but whose womanly faculty made her a staff of strength to support her husband's steps in every hour of trial, trouble, and distress. God help her now, and be to her a tower of strength!

We have spoken of the *last things* in the earthly career of this departed prince of the kingdom of God. But let us not forget that, in the chain of endless causation, there are no last links: there are subtile connections between the life that now is and that which is to come; and, had we the keener perception to trace them, we would learn, doubtless, that the transitions of death do not produce the abrupt and violent changes they seem to involve. Dr. JACOBUS once, in one of his sermons, illustrated the unbroken continuity of the believer's life, begun on earth and prolonged in heaven, by a bold reference to crossing the Allegheny suspension bridge. Looking up from his manuscript, with his countenance all aglow, in his quick, nervous tones, he exclaimed, "What is it for the Christian to die? It is only crossing the suspension bridge. The bridge is wrapped in Pittsburgh mist and smoke. You can't see what lies beyond it. A stranger hesitates to cross it. But, impelled to go forward, he passes over it; and what then? Why, the street goes straight on, with the houses on both sides, and objects in view similar to those he left on this side. He has only changed positions from one side of the river to the other. He has not changed his life, his work, or his inward self. And so death is only crossing the bridge from one city to another, from one street to another. The Christian who is living for God, working for God, and loving God, here on this side of the dark river, continues on the other side of the river to live for God, work for God, and love God. It is a continuous life, continuous work, continuous communion in the love of God!" And so let us think of him now that he himself has crossed the bridge to that other city. He is the same man he was, with the same objects of pursuit before him, — the glory of God in the kingdom of His dear Son; the same motives impelling him to action, — faith, hope, charity; and the same rewards in the experiences of his own soul, for "the kingdom of God" — both here and there — "is within us" (Luke xvii. 21); "for the kingdom of God is righteousness, and peace, and joy in the Holy Ghost" (Rom. xiv. 17). There are no absolute, radical, essential changes wrought in the soul of the Christian by the agency of death. He who consecrated his life to God in childhood, and kept his consecration vows down to the border-land of old age, has passed into a higher sphere from the stage of preparation here; carrying with him his intellectual faculties, his human affections, and his spiritual graces, — not to be destroyed, but purified, elevated, sublimated, and glorified, and still consecrated to God, and employed in His service.

Let us remember, finally, that, though his last acts and words on earth are complete, their results are not yet finished. The Christian, being dead, yet speaketh. And the Christian hero we mourn and commemorate to-day has left words and works that possess in them an indestructible vitality. His contributions to Christian literature, and especially to his favorite department of study, the exposition of inspired Scripture, will continue his influence wherever the English language is read, and, like other writings of that class, can never wholly lose their value. The sermons he preached survive in the hearts of Christian converts, to be preached over again in their lives and words, to exercise converting power in an endless succession of those added to the church, who shall be saved. The instructions of his class-room survive in the ministers they helped to fashion and furnish for the work of extending the gospel to the ends of the world. And the germ-seeds of truth he was sowing day by day in the words he so aptly spoke, — words like apples of gold in baskets of silver, — words in which he knew so well how to condense doctrine in proverbs, and epigrammatic phrases, and antithetical sentences, often humorous, sometimes of the keener-tempered metal of wit, — incisive words, penetrating even dull minds, and inhering in reluctant memories, — those germ-seeds will fructify and reproduce their kindred seed in years and generations and ages yet to come.

Especially must the great work to which he devoted the best part of his life go on, accelerated by the impulse he has given to it. To raise up a pious, educated, and efficient ministry, he employed his intellectual faculties, contributed his large stores of Biblical knowledge, generously distributed his worldly fortune, and labored in prayer night and day; and speaking to us now, with all the appealing power of his own life so unselfishly consecrated to this work, he seems to be exhorting, as in the words of the Apostle Paul to his son Timothy: "And the things that thou hast heard of me, the same commit thou to faithful men, who shall be able to teach others also" (2 Tim. ii. 2). To train "faithful men," "able to teach others," he gave money, prayer, wise counsel, executive ability, intellectual effort, unceasing toil, and, finally, exhausting the nervous power of the physical man by unremitted work, life itself. To us he has left the responsible duty of pursuing with tireless zeal and prompt energy the work he pursued " with his harness on " to the last day of his life. May God make us faithful in fulfilling the trust that in this sudden providence is committed to our hands and hearts, — hands feebler, doubtless, than those now still and helpless! but let us pray that our hearts may not be less warm and enthusiastic than his. Death has chosen a shining mark, and extinguished a burning and a shining light in our beloved church. "But," in the closing words of his inaugural discourse when installed a professor in the Western Theological Seminary, we can say, "The Great Teacher ever lives. And the gracious Master, as Head of the church and Helper of His weak servants, gives the Holy Spirit to them who ask Him."

REMARKS OF THE REV. C. C. BEATTY, D.D.

I DESIRE very particularly in this presence, not only for myself, but as President of the Board of Directors, to express our deep sense of the great loss we have experienced in the death of our senior professor. It has come upon us most unexpectedly, and the loss seems to us irreparable. The Great Head of the Church alone can repair the breach which has been made. We have long tried and known his worth. His long, able, faithful, and successful labors among us have been highly appreciated by us all: he had caused us not only to admire but love him.

He was recently called to another most important position in our Church, as Secretary of the Board of Education, for which he was admirably adapted; and we had some fears that we might lose his valuable services. Indeed, he himself hesitated for a while. He then wrote to me that there were some arguments for a change, as it might give him, in a new position, freshness and energy for action; "and," said he, "if ever I am to make a change from the Seminary, *now* is the time, and *this* is the opportunity." But he decided to remain, and throw himself for life, with all his vigor, into the work of his professorship. Neither he nor any of us thought for how short a time this would be.

But for this quick exit from labor to reward he was not unprepared, in fact or thought or sentiment. We had spoken together, just the day before, of the sudden death of Dr. Howard. Indeed, he several times reverted to it as a subject of his frequent thoughts; and he said, that sudden death, to them that are prepared, was not to be deprecated, but rather desired if God so ordered, as to be "absent from the body is to be present with the Lord." And how frequently since has that excellent form of words come up to my mind, — " The souls of believers are at their death made perfect in holiness, and do immediately pass into glory; their bodies, being still united to Christ, do rest in their graves till the resurrection"! Precious sentiment! blessed truth! "do *immediately* pass into glory!" Yes, he has gone into glory, and why should we grieve? Though absent from us, he is now present with the Lord. Let us follow after.

It was my privilege to spend twenty-four hours with him at his house, but a day before his sudden departure. We had met by appointment, to confer and plan for the future welfare of the Seminary. He was full of interest, fertile in suggestions, and his enthusiastic nature looked forward with hopefulness to its future advancement. Reference was had to the half-century celebration of next spring; "and then, also," said he, "at the same time I shall celebrate my quarter century of connection with it, and we both shall enter upon a new course of usefulness." We shall miss him greatly, not only from the lecture-room, but in regard to his active outside work, in promoting the material interests of the institution in various forms, and for which his executive ability eminently fitted him. He loved the Seminary, and loved to labor for it. Next to the spiritual interests of the kingdom of Christ, the prosperity of this institution lay nearest to his heart.

Did time and the fulness of my heart allow, I should speak of my personal relations so long and so intimately and so happily maintained with this beloved friend and brother and his family; but I must forbear.

To that stricken family — partner, children, relatives — I would say, they have our heartfelt sympathies in their sad bereavement, and our sincere prayers that our and their Heavenly Father, the God of all comfort, may vouchsafe to them the strongest supports and richest consolations of His Holy Spirit. The Lord has called him from us to " go up higher."

SERVICES

IN

THE THIRD PRESBYTERIAN CHURCH,

NEWARK, N.J.

ADDRESS OF THE REV. W. M. PAXTON, D.D.

"And I heard a voice from heaven, saying unto me, Write, Blessed are the dead who die in the Lord." These words seem to assure us of the truth of those beautiful lines of Faber: —

> "There is no place where earth's sorrows
> Are so much felt as up in heaven."

When there is a sorrow down here, there is sympathy up there. Heaven has a care for us in our bitterest trials. A voice comes from the skies, saying, "Write!" But, with our eyes dazzled with the glare of the world, the writing is often invisible to us until the heat of the furnace of affliction brings out the record clear and distinct, and then with what delight we read, "Blessed are the dead who die in the Lord"!

This is a bitter sorrow under which our hearts are oppressed to-day. We all feel it. Our departed brother held so many important positions, and stood in so many different relations, that there is not one of us who in some way or other is not made to feel that this death is a personal grief. A *father* has been taken from the midst of a family, where he was loved, — oh, how tenderly! a *professor*, from a chair which he adorned with his learning; a *teacher*, from the midst of students, who looked to him for guidance in the way of truth; a *minister*, from the pulpit where he attracted so many hearts; and an *author*, from his pen, which he used so successfully in illuminating the word of God. His death is a grief to us, and a loss to the generation which he served.

It only remains with us to recall the points of his useful life; remembering that with us, also, "the time is short."

MELANCTHON W. JACOBUS was born in this city (Newark) on the 19th of September, 1816. He was born again in Bloomfield, N. J., where he was pursuing his preparatory course of academic study. He entered the Sophomore class in Princeton College, at the early age of fifteen; and graduated with the first honor of his class in the year 1834. After a brief interval, he commenced the study of theology in Princeton Seminary, and attained to such proficiency in his studies that, when he graduated, he was retained as an assistant to Prof. Addison Alexander in the department of Hebrew instruction. In the year 1839, he was called and settled in the pastorate of the First Presbyterian Church in the city of Brooklyn, where he remained for a period of eleven years; during which time a large and admiring congregation was attracted by his preaching, and the church advanced to a high degree of prosperity. It was at this time he received the first warning of impaired health. Added to his pastoral and pulpit labors, he had undertaken the preparation of a commentary upon the Gospels, the first volume of which he had already published. The confinement and exhaustion of this accumulated work brought upon him a hemorrhage from the lungs, which rendered it necessary to intermit his labors, and seek refreshment and health in a foreign tour. Accompanied by his wife, he travelled over the Continent of Europe, and then extended his tour to Egypt and the Holy Land, returning by Constantinople and Greece.

It was during this absence that Divine Providence opened to him a door which changed the direction of his after life. The chair of Oriental and Biblical Literature in the Western Theological Seminary in Allegheny City, Pa., was vacant; and the attention of the directors being attracted to his rising fame, both as a preacher and commentator, he was chosen as the man to fill that important position. Upon the nomination of the directors of the Seminary, he was elected to this professorship by the General Assembly, in May, 1851. This call met him in a foreign land. His health had been greatly improved; yet the stress of pulpit labor might endanger his already weakened vocal organs, whilst the comparative quiet of a professor's chair seemed to hold out the hope of continued life. The decision was not difficult to make. He resigned his pastorate in Brooklyn, where many warm friends regretted his loss, and, accepting the chair of Oriental and Biblical Literature, entered upon his duties early in the year 1852.

From that time until his death it was my privilege to know him intimately, and enjoy his confidence. Being then a pastor in the city of Pittsburgh, I was the eye-witness of much of his after life. Knowing the circumstances as I did, I may safely say that no man was ever received with greater cordiality by the citizens of Pittsburgh and Allegheny, and by the large Presbyterian population of Western Pennsylvania. When he preached in the churches, he was listened to with delight; when he commenced his work as a professor, the students gathered around him with admiration; and at synods and presbyteries and conventions, he was popular and influential, a favorite with the elders and with his brethren in the ministry.

His present position was favorable to the accomplishment of the ideal of his life, — the completion of a commentary upon the Sacred Scriptures. His volume upon Matthew had already been published; but now, fresh from the scenes of the Holy Land, and his mind teeming with new thoughts and suggestions, he took up the broken thread of his work, and soon after issued his volume upon Mark and Luke. This was followed by his still more valuable work on the Gospel of John; and, in after years, by the ablest and most scholarly of all his works, — his Commentary upon Acts, and his two volumes upon Genesis. Of the character of these works it is needless for me to speak. They have taken their place among the standard works of the church. Some of them have been republished in England and Scotland. His thoughts upon the Gospels have been reproduced in thousands of Sabbath-schools, and are familiar in many households.

During this period of his professorship, he was providentially drawn into controversy, where his keen intellect and ready learning gave him an easy victory. You may remember that, sometime about the year 1853 or 1854, the Roman Catholic Church in this country began, in an ostentatious way, to claim that the Romish Church is the foster-mother of free institutions. Into this controversy Dr. JACOBUS entered with great freshness and vigor; and, such was his ready learning and skill in argument, that an intelligent public opinion did not hesitate to award him the victory. The bishop whom he fought soon after retired from his episcopal throne, and it was shrewdly suspected by many that this was pursuant to the settled policy of Rome, — not to allow a vanquished champion to remain in honor. It was not precisely with the simple "sling and stone" of David that he slew that Philistine, but rather with the keenness of a scimitar and the flash of a Damascus blade.

But there was another work to which Dr. JACOBUS seemed called of God, which I take pleasure in mentioning, because it rises up before my mind as the most blessed work of his life. It was the authorship of the "Address to the Churches" in the year 1857, which was so greatly blessed of God in promoting the work of revival.

You may remember that the autumn of 1857 was marked by a very severe pecuniary crisis, which was followed, as has often been the case in the history of the church, by a great religious awakening. A convention of the ministers and elders of the five synods, including Western Pennsylvania and Eastern Ohio, met in the First Presbyterian Church in the city of Pittsburg, to pray for the outpouring of God's Spirit upon the churches. On the first day of the meeting, a committee was appointed, of which Dr. JACOBUS was chairman, to draft an address to the churches. The first day of the meeting was not marked by any special interest. Indeed, so dull was the whole proceeding that many of the most anxious and hopeful began to despond. On the second day, toward noon, that remarkable man of God, Dr. Plumer, arose and made a few tender remarks, and concluded by narrating one of the simplest of stories about a little girl who had always observed that her mother comforted herself under all trials by saying, "*Jesus lives.*" One day, seeing her mother bathed in tears, the child ran to her and said, "Mother, mother, is Jesus dead?" The utterance of these words, "Is Jesus dead?" melted the assembly into tears. All hearts seemed broken, stifled sobs could be heard all over the house. It seemed to be the moment when the Spirit of God came down on that assembly. This was immediately followed by the reading of Dr. JACOBUS's Address to the Churches. It had been prepared, as I afterward learned from his correspondence, amid prayers and tears; and, when his burning words fell upon that assembly, the effect was such as cannot well be described. God had prepared him to write. It was baptized with prayer and tears. The thought was so apposite, the appeal so powerful, and the Scripture passages were woven together with such point and power, that it seemed to be the very word of God addressed to every heart. The revival had begun, and God's ministers and elders were baptized for a great work. This Address was published. The ministers carried it home with them; and on the following Sabbath, instead of a sermon, this Address was read in multitudes of pulpits; and, wherever it was read, such a blessing attended it that a great revival followed over all that region of country.

But time will not permit us to continue these personal reminiscences. He has gone, and we mourn his loss. His departure was so sudden that we are stunned and confused by the shock. It seems but yesterday since I saw him in the midst of a joyous marriage scene; but now the tongue that uttered such expressive words of kindness is stilled in death. He died in the faith of those blessed truths which he has so ably expounded and so eloquently preached. Man's sinfulness and Christ's salvation were the great truths which appeared in his whole work as an expositor and preacher. He had a deep sense of his own personal unworthiness in the sight of God, and this led him with a simple faith to accept Christ's righteousness as his only hope. In this confidence he lived and died. And now he has gone —

> "To sit down by the clear
> And crystal waters; he has gone to list
> Isaiah's harp, and David's, and walk
> With Enoch and Elijah and the host
> Of the just men made perfect."

ADDRESS OF THE REV. SAMUEL J. WILSON, D.D.

PERHAPS that which first impressed those who knew Dr. JACOBUS intimately was his wonderful versatility. His mind was many-sided. He was a scholar in the best and truest acceptation of that term, and at the same time he possessed eminent business qualifications. He was a ready and elegant writer, and at the same time a fluent, apt, and eloquent extemporaneous orator. He was an able and accomplished professor, and at the same time a popular and distinguished preacher. He was alike successful as a writer of books, of reviews, and of newspaper articles. He could preach either with or without notes. Few men were happier than he, either in a studied, elaborate address or in an impromptu effusion. He was an indefatigable and enthusiastic student; yet he never became monkish or ascetic, but was always thoroughly awake to the living issues of the times. He was an accomplished ecclesiastic, a ready and an effective debater, and always shone conspicuously on the floor of the Presbytery, the Synod, and the General Assembly; and as the organizer of the scheme of Sustentation in the Presbyterian Church in this country he exhibited extraordinary executive ability. He would have been distinguished in any profession or in any station. He would have occupied a front rank as a merchant, a lawyer, a statesman, or a scientist. Any thing which he undertook to do he did well, and upon all his work he left the distinct impress of a strong individuality. It seemed easy for him to achieve success and distinction in any calling or in any department of human effort. His powers and acquirements were varied, and all of them were at ready and instant command. In his study and lecture-room, he might have been taken for a mere scholar; in the pulpit, he might have been taken for a preacher, and nothing more; in the social circle, he might have been taken for a man who was devoted to society; on the platform, he might have been taken for a popular speaker, and for that alone: yet he passed from each of these divers spheres to the others with perfect ease and naturalness, and was alike distinguished in them all.

Perhaps the next thing which impressed those who knew him well was the rapidity of his intellectual operations. The quickness of his mental movements was wonderful. These movements were as swift as the flight of the eagle, and in their swiftness were sometimes dazzling and bewildering. He was one of the most rapid and facile workers I have ever known. To the rapidity of his intellectual movements both tongue and hand appropriately and sympathetically responded; so that fluent and felicitous speech, and the pen of a ready writer, kept pace with the rapid thought. In this way he was enabled, notwithstanding his ill health, to accomplish an amount of work that was prodigious. With his thoughts coming thick and fast, with a copiousness of fitly chosen words, which never for so much as even a moment failed him, and with a pen which fairly flew across the paper, his achievements in work were amazing.

The fertility of his mind was quite as remarkable as his versatility and as the rapidity of his intellectual operations. He was never tame, he was never dull, he was never commonplace. Upon every subject he was fresh, lively, and suggestive. His mind was a prolific field which abounded with every variety of product. *He brought forth out of his treasure things new and old;* the new being dignified and made attractive by rare and exquisite learning, and the old being beautified by the choicest drapery of expression and imagery. His mind teemed with thoughts, images, and associations, and these were always presented in some new light, with some new tint or shading which a chaste and delicate fancy added to them.

Another characteristic of his was the intense and tireless activity of his mind. He was always busy. His active intellect could not rest. His brain and his hands were always full, and he was constantly projecting new schemes of work and of activity. It so happened, in the providence of God, that for the last ten days of his life I was much in his company. In those ten days, we conversed more on general topics than ordinarily we did in a year. I never knew him to be so full of plans and schemes of work and usefulness. His thoughts ranged over the entire church with its vast interests and enterprises, and it seemed that it would require a hundred lives to carry out all the projects of his fertile brain. With his infirmities of body, ninety-nine men in a hundred would have given up all work; but he seemed only to labor the more intensely, as if admonished that the time was short. His quick eye was on the whole circle of learning, and nothing escaped its notice. He gathered the choicest books around him, read them with avidity, and extracted from them the very quintessence of their contents in so concentrated a form that it was available at any moment and in any emergency. It was impossible to confine his activities to any one particular channel. They would transcend all barriers, and would expend themselves in varied and diverse enterprises. He was always working. His pen never flagged. He worked to the very last.

As a preacher he had few equals. His sermons were scriptural, expository, sound, direct, cogent, clear, fresh, lively, abounding in original thought which was couched in the most beautiful and appropriate language, which was happily at an equal remove from the dry commonplaces of theology on the one hand, and from the dialect of slang and provincialism on the other. He would have adorned any pulpit, and would have edified any congregation. In his knowledge of the English Bible he was, perhaps, absolutely unrivalled. He had memorized not only verses and chapters, but whole books, — indeed, nearly the entire Bible. He always had scriptural quotations pat to the purpose. This greatly enriched his preaching, but it imparted especial unction and impressiveness to his prayers. These prayers of his were unique: none just like them were ever heard; none just like them shall we ever hear again. How inimitable was his paraphrase of the Lord's prayer! The power of the Address, to which Dr. Paxton has so happily and so eloquently referred, consisted largely in the fact that it was drawn directly from the word of God.

His qualities as a pastor were as remarkable as his qualities as a preacher. Affable, genial, and sympathetic, he was alike at home and acceptable in the social circle, in the sick-room, and in the house of mourning.

His scholarship was varied and accurate, and would have adorned any chair. For twenty-three years he performed the duties which belong to the departments of Old and of New Testament exegesis. His connection with the Seminary and my own have been almost contemporaneous. He entered the Seminary as professor a few months before I entered it as a student; and ever since, for all these twenty-five years, as student, as tutor, and as fellow-professor, I have been intimately associated with him, and never for an hour has our friendship been interrupted. We differed, and that, too, where each had cherished and positive convictions. We met often where the angles were sharp, we met where interests clashed, we passed twelve years as pastors of adjoining congregations, and yet never in those twenty-five years was there one moment when we could not meet in perfect cordiality. Dr. JACOBUS had less venom in his composition than any man I ever knew. He never harbored malice. Enmity and spite found no lodging-place in his heart.

As professor, he devoted himself to the interests of the Seminary. He was thoroughly identified with it, and he labored for all its interests. He was very successful in securing patrons for it, and in securing funds for its constantly growing wants. His life for the last quarter of a century has formed a large part of its life and history; and he will be sadly missed, not only in the lecture-room and in the meetings of the Faculty, but in the wider sphere in which the general interests of the institution must be looked after. He died in the harness; he fell on the field; and young men among whom he labored so long carry him to his burial.

His busy, useful life has ended suddenly and mysteriously. If we were the judges, we should say that his life had ended before his work was done: but the purposes of God are inscrutable; and there are infinite reasons lying back of this providence which, if revealed to us, would be perfectly satisfactory to the bereaved Seminary, to these fatherless children, and even to this widowed mother. For this explanation we wait; but he knows it all now. Thank God, he knows it all.

How blessed to be permitted to work up to the very last, without the loss of an hour, without the loss of a single lecture or recitation! The last place I ever saw him alive was at his desk in the lecture-room. He finished the work of the day; and, before the bell summoned to duty the next day, he had entered upon a higher service in heaven. How blessed to fall asleep in Jesus, without seeing death or tasting its bitterness!

When we have spoken of the public life of the deceased, of his professorial, of his pastoral, and of his ecclesiastical work, of his books and his literary productions, we have only given the exterior of his life. To describe him fully, we should have to intrude within an enclosure which is too sacred to be exposed to view here. Dr. JACOBUS was only truly and fully known at his home, in his family, as husband and father. To those who thus knew him best, all his honors and titles sound hollow and empty compared with the more sacred titles of husband and father. On this hallowed ground I shall not dare to tread. We stand in the outer court. Within the sanctuary are the golden candlesticks, the table of shew-bread, and the altar of incense.

ADDRESS OF THE REV. WM. M. ADAMS, D.D.

THE death of a Christian minister! At how many graves has he stood ere he reached his own! Into how many homes stricken with sorrow has he entered, with ministries of consolation, before his own home was made desolate by his departure! How often has he preached to his fellow-men concerning death, and Him who is the Resurrection and the Life, before he himself passed into the great mystery of dissolution!

In such a presence it is that we gather our best lessons as to the true value of life. Two aspects of humanity are brought together by the inspired apostle. "All flesh is as grass, and all the glory of man as the flower of grass. The grass withereth, and the flower thereof falleth away; but the word of the Lord endureth for ever. And this is the word which by the gospel is preached unto you." In one aspect, what so frail and evanescent as a human life? In another, even as associated with the word of God, and that destiny to which it points, what so sublime and imperishable? It is the province of every Christian minister to be connected with his fellow-men in those matters which relate to what is divine and immortal. As he passes from the world when his work is finished, we recall the fact that his influence never can die. It surpasses our power of computation. It has given stimulus to thought, and direction to character. You may put in order the number of public services he has rendered, enumerate the sabbaths and the sermons of his official career; but who can measure that invisible influence which he has exerted in the comparisons and judgments and purposes of hundreds and thousands who have been led into a religious life by his persuasion and fidelity! Blessed, indeed, is he who, dying in the Lord, is permitted to see the long succession of good results which follow his faithful work in the ministry of Christ. If I may be permitted to paraphrase the language of Mr. Coleridge concerning a distinguished teacher, I would say: "When I would frame to myself the most inspiriting representation of future bliss which my mind is capable of comprehending, it would be embodied to me in the idea of a Christian minister receiving, at some distant period, the appropriate reward of his earthly labors, when thousands and ten thousands of glorified spirits, whose reason and conscience had through his efforts been unfolded, shall sing the song of their own redemption, and, pouring forth praise to God and to their Saviour, shall repeat his 'new name' in heaven, give thanks for his earthly virtues, as the chosen instruments of divine mercy to themselves, and not seldom perhaps turning their eye towards him, as from the sun to its image in the fountain, with secondary gratitude and the permitted utterance of a human love."

The death of a Christian scholar! Superficial minds, judging according to sense, might regard the life of a student, delving in books and making books, as of small account in this great and noisy world. But the wheels which make the noise as they grind the grain and saw the lumber are put in motion by the stream, which has its beginning in the hills, and flows quietly along through the meadows, attracting no attention to itself. The author of a good book is the true Methuselah: he lives a thousand years who excites and informs and directs other minds for generations after he has gone from the sight of men. Specially true is this of the good and the great men who have given their lives to the elucidation of the Holy

Scriptures. Generations pass along over the earth, customs change, nations perish; but the word of the Lord abideth for ever; and he who writes any thing which helps men to a better understanding of the Bible has a share in the immortality of that book which he illustrates. Judge not that a Christian scholar passes a life of idleness and waste; for

> "A drop of ink
> Falling, like dew, upon a thought
> Produces that which makes thousands, perhaps millions, think."

The *sudden* death of a Christian minister! Smitten when in full armor in the midst of vigorous duty! So Chalmers died. Lying down at night in apparent health, with the implements for writing within easy reach of his hand, that he might work when first he woke, and at the early dawn his liberated soul exclaimed, "Let me go, for the morning breaketh." So died Albert Barnes and Nicholas Murray; so died our common friend Dr. William D. Howard, at whose funeral, three weeks before his own, Dr. JACOBUS so tenderly officiated. Let us dismiss all speculations and preferences as to the time and mode of our departure, since concerning these we have no responsibility. With one thing only are we charged,— always to be ready. Death never can be sudden to one who lives so mindful of his exposure to it that he may be said, in the language of the apostle, to die daily. Never can it be unexpected to him who is well prepared for its coming. May God help us all so to live that we may adopt the words of the pious Baxter: "Lord, when thou wilt, how thou wilt, where thou wilt; be it only that I am ready."

My personal associations with Dr. JACOBUS became intimate for the first time in connection with those negotiations which resulted in the reunion of the two branches of the Presbyterian Church. He was the moderator of his own assembly at the time when the vote was taken to consummate the union. Thrown much into his society at that time, it gives me pleasure to recall his uniform urbanity and wisdom and catholic, Christian temper. Several associated with us on those committees of conference have already gone. Surely they do not regret, in their abodes of glory, what they did in the cause of Christian unity and love. Should I adopt the thought of Leighton, — that in the presence of death all earthly distinctions fade out of sight, even as all colors are alike in the dark, — the association might well be regarded as too sombre. Rather would we say that, in the light of heaven and in the presence of our Lord, all the petty differences which divide and separate on earth are lost for ever in the glory of a common relationship to God and the Lamb!

Rapidly are the servants of Christ passing to their eternal home. To many this world is growing lonesome; but heaven becomes more and more home-like and populous as companions and colaborers are removed thither. We understand better, every time that a familiar friend is translated to that world of joy, the words of inspiration, "We are come to the general assembly and church of the first-born which are written in heaven, and to the spirits of just men made perfect."

> "Ten thousand times ten thousand,
>   In sparkling raiment bright,
> The armies of the ransomed saints
>   Throng up the steeps of light.
> 'Tis finished, all is finished,
>   Their fight with death and sin:
> Fling open wide the golden gates,
>   And let the victors in.
> Oh, then what rapturous greetings
>   On Canaan's happy shore!
> What knitting severed friendships up
>   Where partings are no more!"

ADDENDA.

DR. JACOBUS AND THE SCHEME OF SUSTENTATION.

IT seems proper that some supplemental reference should here be made to the services of Dr. JACOBUS in connection with the General Assembly's Scheme of Ministerial Sustentation, of which he was the earnest advocate and zealous promoter, and of which he was for three years the efficient secretary. What here follows upon that subject is simply condensed from his annual reports presented to the Assembly; and is designed to exhibit, in as compact form as possible, his views of the magnitude and importance of the work, the considerations by which he defended the necessity of a sustentation agency, and the actual results achieved. No eulogy or encomium is attempted, nor any comment offered. The arguments which he employed are simply recited, and the facts are allowed to speak for themselves.

A growing concern had been felt for years in the Presbyterian Church on the subject of the inadequate support of the ministry, with all the privations, anxieties, and discouragements which it occasioned to ministers themselves and their families, as well as the damage thence resulting to the church itself, since it seriously curtailed the amount and impaired the efficiency of ministerial work, and proved the fruitful source of other alarming and increasing evils. The conviction was general that some adequate remedy must be devised, and ought to be applied. Great expense was incurred in educating men for the ministry. A disabled ministers' fund was provided for those who were worn-out in the service: but a large proportion of those who were actually engaged in doing the work of the church received, instead of a generous support, a miserable and scanty pittance; and existing methods of relief were quite unable to correct this grievous wrong. This matter engaged the attention of the first assembly of the reunited church in 1870; and a committee, of which Dr. JACOBUS was chairman, was appointed to consider and report upon the question of sustentation. A resolution was also referred to this committee, directing inquiry to be made into the stipends of ministers; and the results laid before the next General Assembly, with suggestions as to the best means of raising the smaller stipends.

Inquiries were accordingly addressed to all who were in charge of churches, whether pastors or stated supplies. Out of the entire number (2,729), answers were received from 2,100. Of these, but 852 received salaries of $1,000 or upwards; 1,248 received under $1,000 (of whom 432 were pastors, and 816 stated supplies). There were 909 who received less than $800: of these, 281 were pastors, and

628 stated supplies. And 622 received less than $600: of these, 145 were pastors, and 477 stated supplies. Of the 629 who were not reported, more than 200 were home missionaries: so that the general average would not have been materially affected if all had been heard from. In the language of the committee: "These figures represent startling and saddening facts, calling loudly for action." "Here is a large class of educated men, with cultivated tastes, and with wives of refinement, used to comfortable living, who endure drudgery, and suffer hardships and privations which they would shame to tell: their children growing up with meagre facilities of schooling; the minister, who should owe no man any thing, unable to worry through the year without debt, always under the harrow, wasting his best energies in making ends meet."

Hence the increasing instability of the pastoral office: hosts of candidates flocking to every desirable vacancy, and bringing the ministry into contempt; the multiplication of stated supplies, one thousand of our working ministers standing in this equivocal and temporary relation, — a relation unknown to our constitution; the great number of unemployed ministers and vacant churches (out of 4,238 ministers on our roll, only 2,700 at the utmost being in any ministerial charge, and only 1,625 being pastors; while out of the 4,526 churches on our lists, more than one-fifth are vacant); preachers without charge accumulating in large places, and fearing to go to destitute regions; the enforced secularization of the ministry (men ordained to preach the gospel, and who, by divine ordinance, should live of the gospel, constrained by sheer lack of bread for their needy households to turn aside to secular pursuits, and, abandoning sacred functions altogether, or devoting to them but a fraction of their time and strength); young men of talent and piety deterred from entering the ministry, and drawn aside to other avocations which offer at least a comfortable living; the popular impression created, and the sentiment actually advocated publicly, that the ranks of the ministry are full, and even overcrowded, notwithstanding the spiritual wastes that everywhere abound, and the fact that our Lord's injunction, "Preach the gospel to every creature," is utterly unfulfilled.

This state of things, it was urged, betrays a deficiency in our existing methods. It is not to be traced to incompetency in the ministry. Whatever may be true in individual cases, though some may have mistaken their calling, so sweeping and cruel a charge cannot be brought, with any show of justice or truth, against this large body of faithful and devoted men, — men who will compare favorably, on the whole, with the ministry of any church or of any land, or with their brethren in our own church more favorably circumstanced; and who are ready and anxious, if the opportunity were afforded, to do good service for the church and for their

Lord. This cannot, with any reason or fairness, be treated as a purely commercial question, and allowed to adjust itself by the law of supply and demand; as though a preacher were worth what he will fetch, and will fetch what he is worth, and a poorly-paid minister were for that reason to be subjected to the suspicion that he is not worth a living salary, and is unfit for his work.

It was further urged that, according to the Presbyterian doctrine of the unity of the church, there is an obligation resting upon the entire body to secure to the faithful ministry a competent support. "There is a field for every true and faithful minister of Christ in this broad land; and the church ought to sustain him in his field, as much if he be at work in America as if he were at work in India or in China." "Although the particular congregation which is served by the living preacher is, in a sense, more immediately obligated, as being more directly interested and obliged, yet the church at large is surely bound to secure a maintenance for her ministers, as ordained by her for the work at large, and as belonging to her necessary apparatus for evangelizing the world."

This duty has in fact been recognized by the church from the beginning, and through her Home Mission Board she is extending aid to 1,200 out of her 2,700 working ministers. But this very circumstance calls for serious thought: a large proportion of the churches assisted by the Board of Home

Missions are in the older States and in long-settled districts. Many of them have been in this state of dependence for many years, and are making no visible progress toward self-support. And, then, the entire number that must be aided is so considerable that the amount which can be afforded to each is necessarily small, — much smaller in a multitude of cases than the presbyteries and churches ask for, and smaller than the Board would gladly grant if they had the means at their disposal to do so. The inquiry hence arose, whether this important and indispensable arm of our church might not be materially strengthened, and the work which it is now vigorously yet vainly struggling to overtake be essentially aided by the incorporation of a new feature in our system of relief. While the Board is left to continue the same method as heretofore, and to accomplish all that it is possible for it to do, cannot a new agency be devised, auxiliary to it, which shall relieve the Board of a portion of its work; and, by applying a special stimulus to such mission churches as are prepared for it, and granting them larger aid for a limited period, afford a competent support at once to a number of deserving pastors, whose hands will thus be strengthened and their hearts encouraged, and their churches put upon a process which will soon issue in self-support, and thus place them beyond the need of further assistance? The larger outlay, for a brief term, in churches of this description, would be true economy, if it could be so applied as to impart a new stimulus to them, and they could be thereby roused to bestir themselves to do their best to stand alone, instead of sinking down contented in a state of permanent dependence. This method can then be successively applied to ever-widening circles. As churches thus effectively relieved are in succession lifted out of their state of needy dependence into the condition of self-support, the funds thus released could be in turn extended to others, with the hope that, in no very long time, the entire body of the hard-working and poorly-paid pastors throughout our whole church could be reached, and a decent maintenance afforded to them all; while the Home Board, thus relieved, could be extending its arm of aid further and further into the regions beyond, and reclaiming the outlying wastes and desolations.

This attempt to raise the salaries of the underpaid ministry to the point of a comfortable maintenance as speedily as possible, and to bring the mission churches up to the condition of self-support, was, it was constantly urged, to be associated with and furthered by the conjunction of contiguous weak charges under one pastorate. It was no part of the scheme to further the multiplication of separate charges in districts, or under circumstances where they manifestly could never be sustained, or to burden the church at large with the support of two or more separate pastors in the midst of a population which could be adequately served by a single pastor whom they could maintain themselves. The mistake of dissociating churches which had been and ought to be joined together may sometimes have been inadvertently committed in the subsequent management of this scheme, and there may have been other errors of judgment arising from imperfect information; but these were no part of the scheme itself. And no one would be more ready to admit or to correct such errors, if they existed, than those who were charged with its administration.

Influenced by such considerations as these, the General Assembly adopted the scheme of sustentation which was proposed; appointing a special committee to take it in charge, and electing Dr. JACOBUS to be its secretary, — a post which he accepted and held, so long as he retained it at all, on the condition that he should receive no salary for his services. The object attempted was to enable such churches as came into the scheme to raise their salaries to $1,000. In order to do this, the church must itself make up at least $500 toward this amount; and the sum raised for this purpose by the church must amount to not less than $7.30 per member; the minister in charge must be regularly settled as a pastor; the church must contribute, in advance, to the Sustentation Fund one-twentieth of their share of the salary, and must make systematic contributions to all the boards of the church; and both the necessities of the church, and its satisfactory compliance with all the requirements of the scheme, must be regularly certified by the Presbytery.

Each congregation aided was thus incited to do its utmost for its own support: it was trained to take an interest in all the causes of benevolence conducted by our church; the formation of the pastoral relation was encouraged, instead of the loose connection of stated supply; contiguous churches were encouraged to unite, in order to avail themselves more readily of the benefits offered by the scheme; and the regular growth of membership would, in a few years, by the very conditions of the aid furnished, place the church beyond the need of receiving it further.

Several months were necessarily spent in getting the scheme fairly started: but in the first annual report to the General Assembly, in 1872, the Secretary was able to state, that 748 churches had contributed $41,073.52 to the cause of sustentation; and meanwhile the receipts of the Board of Home Missions, instead of being diminished thereby, were $30,000 more than ever before; and it was, in addition, relieved of the support of 72 ministers transferred to this scheme. 114 applications for aid had been granted, amounting to $18,212.92; and 61 stated supplies had been made pastors; and the minutes of the Assembly for that year show an increase of 150 installations over either of the two previous years, with no increase of dissolutions. The report further states: "Many churches testify that the people have done far more for the minister, and for all the boards of the church, than would have been possible under any other arrangement: *e.g.*, 'Our people have done fifty per cent more for the salary, and one hundred per cent more for the boards, than ever they had done.' . . . The scheme set on foot a new movement. Many churches advanced their salary to $1,000, without our aid; many stated supplies hastened to become pastors; churches which were below the minimum increased their salary, so as to come under the scheme. If, as now seems, this movement is to go largely forward along the whole line of our weak churches, there will be a general lifting up of large numbers, and that according to a scheme which will not allow of dependence upon the church funds for an indefinite time. They will here be put upon a sliding scale towards speedy self-sustentation."

The second annual report to the Assembly, in 1873, states that, during the past year, 1,269 churches had contributed $60,184.20, which, with the former balance, gave a total of $83,044.80; 308 ministers had been taken under the scheme, and $70,858.40 disbursed; 200 home missionaries had, by the operation of the plan, been settled as pastors, and the funds of the Home Board relieved to that extent. "Reports have been received from 200 churches under our scheme, which show their total of contributions to the boards to be $20,000, as compared with $6,000 during the same period previous. Most of these churches had been under the Home Mission Board, which is thus doubly relieved by transfer of the churches, and by increase of funds from this source and by this means. In the amount raised by these churches themselves for the salaries of their ministers, the increase is to $110,000, from $85,000 previous to sustentation. These figures show a solid gain of $39,000 under this regimen. And, estimating for the remainder (one-half more) in the same proportion, we would have $58,500 of gain in salaries and offerings to the boards beyond the same period previous." And testimonies of the strongest and most decided character are recited, from various synods, presbyteries, and individual churches, to the salutary and effective working of the scheme. And the General Assembly declared "that this scheme is one of the very highest importance to our church; that its administration has been prudent and able; and that it should no longer be regarded in the light of an experiment, but fully established as a part of the settled policy of the church." The agitation of the subject, also, bore its indirect fruits; the Assembly's minutes showing an increase, during the year, of over half a million of dollars in the column of ministers' salaries.

The next year was, in all respects, a most trying one, and calculated to put the scheme to the severest test; both because of the financial panic, and because the report of the Consolidation Committee, published some time before the meeting of the Assembly, had suggested a discontinuance of the Sustentation Committee as a separate agency, and thus led to a greater diminution of the receipts in the last two months of the year than had previously been occasioned by the monetary stringency. In spite of these depressing circumstances, however, the third report, in 1874, mentions 266 pastorates under the scheme, 13 of which had become self-sustaining; $51,758.03 had been received, which, with the surplus of the previous year, gave a total of $63,944.43; and $67,388.63 had been paid out, leaving an indebtedness of $3,444.20. The March payments were in arrears about $4,000; and on the next pay-day, June 1st, there would be a further liability of $14,500.[1] Of the churches aided by the scheme, full reports had been received from 155: from which it appeared that they had raised, during the year, $44,506 more for ministers' salaries than they had done prior to sustentation, and $9,365 more for contributions to the several boards of the church; making a total gain of $53,871. If those not fully reported were estimated in the same proportion, there would result a total gain of $92,800.

Dr. JACOBUS resigned his official connection with the scheme at that time; and the Assembly recognized the value and the disinterestedness of his services in the following resolution: —

"*Resolved*, That the thanks of the Assembly are due, and are hereby cordially tendered, to the Rev. M. W. JACO-

---

[1] At the time of its transfer to the Board of Home Missions, in the month of June, the deficiency amounted to $31,014.35, according to the statement of the Board.

BUS, D.D., Secretary and Treasurer of the Sustentation Committee, who has served the church in this capacity for three years, with distinguished ability and faithfulness and without salary."

It may be safely said, that no enterprise in which our church has ever engaged met with more marked favor, or achieved a higher success in so brief a period. There were diversities of judgment in respect to some of the details of the scheme, and opposition was encountered in certain quarters. But the facts, which stand on permanent record, abundantly demonstrate the feasibility of the scheme in the hands of a man of the requisite executive ability, who has faith in its working, and who means to make it succeed.

LETTERS, RESOLUTIONS, &c.

From a Member of his Church in Pittsburgh.

ALLEQUIPPA, Nov. 6.

MY DEAR MRS. JACOBUS, — I have hesitated about writing to you, lest the expression of my grief should renew your own, and be less kind than silence. My thoughts are constantly with you, and I feel that I must express something of the love and sympathy I bear you. My dear, dear Mrs. Jacobus, if *I* am left desolate and sorrowing, how will *you* bear this bereavement? You know all that *I* have lost in the death of your dear husband, — a most true and faithful pastor, wise counsellor, sympathizing in my sorrows, and ever ready to aid me by the kindest, wisest advice; a most honored friend, — yes, he allowed me to call him such, though the title I ever felt to be the greatest condescension from one such as he. Ah! how can I spare him? Where can I ever find an ear so willing and a voice so wise? Whose prayers for me and mine can ever replace his? I trust that my love for my dear pastor will lead me to honor him by a renewed consecration of myself to the service of the Master whom he so loved, and to whose glory he devoted his life and talents. Already he seems to speak to me across the great river that lies between us; his former words come back with all their winning earnestness; and, for his dear sake, I *will* make new efforts to serve my God faithfully. With a heart full of sympathy, believe me

Your loving and sorrowing friend,

E. S. B.

From a Member of his Brooklyn Church.

BALTIMORE, Nov. 2.

MY DEAR FRIEND, — I have just laid down the paper containing the sad intelligence of the death of our beloved former pastor. I do not write with even the faintest hope of soothing your deep, overwhelming sorrow; but to assure you that in *our* home there is deep sympathy with you, and to express, with numberless others, our sincere affection and genuine, heartfelt esteem, and even reverence, for that dear one whose departure has left an aching void in the hearts of so many. As I read the account of his useful life and his endearing qualities, my heart responded, "So true, so true, is it all!" How often has my memory dwelt so lovingly on that precious visit to us here during that meeting of the

Northern General Assembly! Those delightful days of sweet Christian intercourse can never be forgotten. The evenings were warm; and, as we sat in the darkened parlor at the hour of worship, there was no need of the written word for him who conducted our devotions for us. A psalm of David was repeated so sweetly that the charm of it was enhanced; and then the earnest petitions which followed made us feel as though we were indeed in a little sanctuary below. In your grief is no bitterness, except that it will cost us a bitter pang to surrender our dearest treasures, even into the loving arms of our Redeemer.

Yours, with the same old love,
S. H. A.

From the President of the Board of Directors of the Seminary.

STEUBENVILLE, Oct. 28.

MY DEAR, DEAR, AFFLICTED FRIEND, — I have just received your telegram. Oh, how sudden and unexpected! I feel that my best, dearest friend on earth has gone from me; but gone to his Saviour and Lord. I had never thought of his going before me; but such is the divine will, and I bow to it. He had spoken to me more than once of Dr. Howard's death, and the effect on his mind; but we both agreed that the time and way made but little difference when we are prepared. He was fully so. How has glory succeeded to the darkness of this world! He had many, many friends who will deplore their loss in his sudden departure from among them. It will give a shock to our whole church; but our dear Seminary is the greatest loser, after his own family. Accept the sympathy of my stricken heart for you and all the children.

   Your affectionate friend,
        CHARLES C. BEATTY.

From the President of the Board of Trustees of the Seminary.

          PITTSBURGH, Nov. 8.

MRS. DR. JACOBUS: —

My dear Madam, — I thought, on my return home from Newark, I would see you, and express my sympathy in this hour of your sorrow and bereavement; but illness prevents me. Dr. JACOBUS was one of my dearest and most beloved friends. He is gone: God has taken him. He served his day and generation faithfully, and, as far as it is possible for man to do, he fulfilled the whole duty of man. The family's loss, the church's loss, the Seminary's loss, is great beyond measure, and to us irreparable. He has finished his labors: his works will follow him. He has received the crown; and nothing is left undone by him for us to do but to bless and thank God for his lifetime labors of love, and for his shining example in the church and the world. We have received all by his hands from God, as a faithful shepherd. In an hour when we thought not, God has taken him from us. Our duty to God is plain, — that we cling closer to his God and our God, and say, "Thy will be done."

Very truly yours,
JAMES LAUGHLIN.

From another Member of his Brooklyn Church.

NEW YORK CITY, Nov. 10, 1876.

MY DEAR MRS. JACOBUS, — You, of course, learned that Mrs. Dunham and myself attended the funeral services of your dear husband. It was a sad, sad blow to us all. To say we sorrow does not express our feelings. There was no man living for whom I entertained greater respect, and, I may add, no one out of our immediate family circle whom I loved and revered as I did the doctor. It was only a few days prior to his decease I was looking over several of his kind and affectionate letters, all showing his intense interest and anxiety for my soul's salvation. He was a true friend. Mrs. D. joins me in very affectionate remembrance to you and your family.

Very truly,
W. S. D.

From an Old Seminary Friend.

UTICA, N. Y., Nov. 4, 1876.

MY DEAR MADAM, — It is not meet for a stranger to intermeddle with grief like yours; but my very long-long-ago acquaintance with your husband, formed during our student life at Princeton, and while seated at the same table, under the roof of the Misses Brearley, the high regard and warm affection I then formed for him, and which the many years past since never impaired, and the relations into which we were brought at an intensely interesting and most momentous period in the history of our church, impel me to take the liberty of saying that I share your bereavement; and that, if sympathy could comfort you in the least, my heart is full of it. Endurance and duty remain to us here; and let me say for your encouragement that there may be found an untried sweetness in them. Passing under the rod is delicious indeed; and what a satisfaction there is in letting the Lord work out his designs by us, even though it be by rugged paths and heavy crosses! But, with all the rewards and enjoyments of patience and service, your eyes must turn now from earth to heaven. The springs from which you have so largely drank are broken up; but a little way on is the "pure river of water of life, clear as crystal, proceeding out of the throne of God and of the Lamb."

Yours most sincerely,

P. H. FOWLER.

From a Ministerial Friend.

ALBANY, Nov. 1, 1876.

MRS. JACOBUS: —

Dear Madam, — I am deeply afflicted in your great affliction, of which I was apprised in looking over the *New York Tribune* last evening. None could know your husband without esteeming and loving him. I regard my acquaintance and intercourse with him, though far less than I could have desired, a great privilege; and the reminiscence will ever be cherished lovingly. It is a great pleasure to me to remember what a distinguished career of Christian usefulness your dear husband has been enabled to pursue; how much good he has done for Christ and for his fellow-men; how amiable in character, courteous in manners, and blameless in life. And, if it be a pleasure to me thus to remember him, how much more to you, my afflicted friend? Do not think of him as dead. He is not dead, but living, enjoying more of life, and a nobler life, than he ever enjoyed here. May the peace of God, which passeth understanding, keep your heart and mind, through Christ Jesus; and may the grace of God be sufficient for you, and for the whole circle of family and relatives; to whom convey the sympathy and condolence of Your sincere friend,

JAMES R. BOYD.

From an Old Student.

PLAINFIELD, Nov. 5.

DEAR MRS. JACOBUS, — Just let me say that, among all the letters you are doubtless receiving, no one of them conveys a truer sympathy than that which I would by these lines have you know is in my inmost heart for you. Since the death of my old friend and pastor, Dr. Chambers, I have felt nothing so deep and strong as the emotions which possessed me when, on Wednesday, I stood by that coffin in Newark. It seemed so hard to look on that dear, familiar face, and think I should see it no more. The memories of all my pleasant intercourse with him in the days of my student life, and in later days also, came thronging in upon me, together with thoughts of what a large place he filled in the work of the church, and what a great vacancy was made by his taking away. How little did I think a year ago that those beautiful lines he wrote on Mr. Newkirk's death would thus soon be applicable to himself. Ah! what "hosannas to the Lamb, with raptures all untold," he has been singing this past week in the home above the skies!

In tenderest sympathy, yours affectionately,

JOHN C. BLISS.

From an Early Student.

PITTSBURGH, Oct. 30, 1876.

MY DEAR MRS. JACOBUS, — I wish it were in my power to say a word to comfort your heart in your great sorrow. If human sympathy could relieve your anguish, I am sure you have it from multitudes of God's dear people throughout the world. The whole church is afflicted in the loss of our dear Dr. JACOBUS. But our loss is his gain. Though his death was so sudden and startling, yet it was so fitting and beautiful! He had finished his work, and God took him. "Not lost, but gone before." Done with bearing the cross, already he wears the crown.

With a profound sense of personal obligation to your dear husband, now in glory,

I am, very sincerely yours,

W. T. BEATTY.

From a Ministerial Friend.

DOWNINGTOWN, PA., Oct. 31, 1876.

MY DEAR MRS. JACOBUS, — I am grieved beyond expression to hear of the death of Dr. JACOBUS. The day before this intelligence reached me, I was engaged for some time in studying one of the doctor's commentaries, and, as I sat with the book in my hand, I fancied I could see the face and form of my beloved friend, and I seemed to receive instruction more from him than from the printed page. Frequently, I recall the days I was privileged to spend in your happy home. How much I enjoyed those visits it is impossible to tell. As we sat in the house, and as we walked or rode to and from church or presbytery, the doctor's conversation was to me a continual feast. He was always agreeable, interesting, and instructive, and, at times, full of humor. It seemed to me that he had read every book worth reading; that he had knowledge of every person of any prominence or distinction; that he was informed of every question or movement in church or state; and that he was as familiar with the Bible as with the alphabet. It was always a wonder to me how he could accomplish as much as he did. While discharging, with distinguished ability, the responsible duties of professor, he did not fail to meet all the requirements of his office as pastor of the Central Church. And yet he found time to write valuable commentaries, for which there has been a great and increasing demand in this country and in Great Britain; and he attended religious conventions, and meetings of Presbytery, Synod, and the General Assembly, and took an active part in their discussions and proceedings. His was indeed a busy life. He was a good and faithful servant of our blessed Lord and Master, and great will be his joy and reward in heaven. I sympathize deeply with you and your family in your sore bereavement. Not many know better than I what a heavy and irreparable loss you have sustained. Others feel the loss sustained by the Seminary and the church, which he loved and served so well. Many will lament the death of Dr. JACOBUS. Although he is dead, yet we are confident that he will not be forgotten; and that his influence, works, and example will be perpetuated. Very sincerely yours,

FRANCIS J. COLLIER.

From a Ministerial Friend.

PHILADELPHIA, Oct. 31.

MY DEAR MRS. JACOBUS, — I am well aware that you are in a condition of grief that should make a stranger hesitate to meddle; but I cannot resist the desire to express my great astonishment and grief, and to assure you of my sympathy. My relations to your husband were most intimate and pleasant, and my regard for him the highest. I cannot forget the deep interest he has always manifested in me, and his continued kindness to me through my entire ministry. The public esteem, of which you have so many assurances, cannot compensate for the great loss experienced in the inner sacred home-circle, where the darkness is so thick; but it must be a gratification to know that your home-treasure was so valued in the world, and, more than all, in the church of Christ.

He has done a great work for Christ, and left a name most honorable in our Presbyterian household. There must be a sweet rest for a servant who toils so long and toils so well in the vineyard. The Master must have given a warm welcome in the Father's house to one who believed so firmly, and was so helpful to the faith of others. I greatly regretted his not coming to Philadelphia. It seems as if God had kept him for this better change, and shown His grace by translating him from the midst of many friends. Please accept this word of tribute and sympathy from one who feels indebted to your husband and laments his loss. May the precious Saviour, whose preciousness he so well knew and could so richly proclaim, comfort you and your fatherless children, and keep you in His grace till He brings you to his glory and to your dead.

Very affectionately, your friend in Christ,

CHARLES A. DICKEY.

Extract from Minutes of the Faculty of Western Theological Seminary.

ON Saturday, Oct. 28, at 7 o'clock A.M., suddenly died almost without premonition, our senior professor, Rev. MELANCTHON WILLIAMS JACOBUS, D.D., LL.D., having faithfully and successfully discharged his duties as a member of this Faculty for nearly a quarter of a century.

We, his stricken brethren, would leave on record, in our minutes, this simple expression of our love to him; of our unspeakable sense of his loss to our Seminary; of our thankfulness for all that God has accomplished for the cause of Christ, through the instrumentality of this honored servant; of our prayer for grace to bear the increased burden that devolves on us, by the removal of our head and chief, who so efficiently sustained all the interests, and was laboriously active in the general management of the affairs, of this institution; and of our tender and prayerful sympathy for his bereaved family, with whom we weep as fellow-mourners.

Action of the Board of Directors of the Western Theological Seminary.

WHEREAS, since the last meeting of this Board it has pleased the Head of the church to remove by death the Rev. MELANCTHON W. JACOBUS, D.D., LL.D., who, since 1851, has, with great distinction, filled the chair of Hebrew and Biblical Literature and Exegesis, the members of the Board feel themselves called upon to give expression to their feelings under this great bereavement, in the following minute: —

The Rev. Dr. M. W. JACOBUS was elected by the General Assembly of 1851 to the professorship which he has fulfilled for nearly a quarter of a century, with such distinguished ability as not only to give the best benefits of culture to the students from time to time under his care, but also to attract the confidence of the church and the country to the Seminary. The fruits of his scholarship and extended study have also largely appeared in the valuable commentaries upon various books of Scripture which he has given to the public. At the same time, his active service in behalf of the benevolent work of our church, as well as in his able ministry of the gospel, have made a record which cannot be obliterated. He was called away from the midst of his work, and while he was maturing plans for the advanced welfare of our beloved institution. His extensive reputation shall still be cherished as a part of the rich inheritance of the Western Theological Seminary. His spirit of consecration to the Master's work leaves no doubt, in those who have been associated with him, that he is now with the Lord.

A true copy:

W. T. BEATTY, *Secretary.*

Resolutions of the Board of Trustees of the Western Theological Seminary.

Resolved, 1. That in the death of Rev. M. W. JACOBUS, D.D., LL.D., the senior professor of the Seminary, we recognize the hand of an all-wise and merciful Providence; and, while we deeply mourn our loss in the removal of one whom we have learned to love and esteem most highly, not only because of his ripe scholarship and marked adaptability to the duties of his chair, but because of the great excellence of his character, we would, nevertheless, submissively bow to the will of Him whom we seek to serve and unto whom we humbly look for grace and wisdom in all our ways.

Resolved, 2. That we hereby tender the widow and children of our deceased brother our warmest sympathies in this time of sorrow, and beg to commend them to the care and mercy of our common Saviour.

Resolutions of the Presbytery of Allegheny.

THE Presbytery of Allegheny being in session on the day of the funeral of Dr. M. W. JACOBUS, appointed a committee to prepare appropriate resolutions expressive of their views on this sad occasion. These are submitted as follows:—

1. *Resolved*, That, in view of the solemn lessons of Providence in the sudden death of Rev. MELANCTHON W. JACOBUS, D.D., LL.D., at so short an interval after the equally sudden death of Rev. William D. Howard, D.D., the members of this Presbytery feel called upon to give most earnest heed to these impressive admonitions to quicken our diligence in our Master's work, inasmuch as we know not in what hour we too may be called to meet the Son of man.

2. *Resolved,* That we tender our sincere sympathy to our sister Presbytery of Pittsburgh in the loss of two of the most eminent and useful of their members within so short a time; also, to the Directors and Faculty of the Western Theological Seminary, in being deprived of the valuable services of a professor so eminently qualified for his work.

3. *Resolved,* That we do especially express our most cordial sympathy with the bereaved families of our brethren, Howard and Jacobus, and would commend them to the God of all grace and consolation, who doeth all things well; while we would encourage ourselves and them with the assurance that the Lord had need of these His servants, who had so well done their work on earth, that He may employ them in higher and better service in His upper kingdom.

Action of the Central Church of Pittsburgh.

With profound sorrow this congregation has heard of the death of its former pastor, Dr. Melancthon Williams Jacobus, who died suddenly at his residence in Allegheny City, on the morning of Oct. 28, 1876; and, while we bow in submission to the will of "Him who doeth all things well," we desire to pay a proper tribute to the memory of the eminent and beloved deceased.

In the death of Dr. Jacobus the ministry has lost one

of its brightest lights, the church one of its boldest and most successful defenders, his family its honored head, and society a devout Christian. His life was an eminently successful one. Graduating at an early age, and with high honors, at Princeton College, he shortly thereafter entered the ministry in the Presbyterian Church, and preached and labored in an Eastern congregation with great acceptance for many years, and until he was elected professor in the Western Theological Seminary of our neighboring city of Allegheny. He came amongst us in the maturity and vigor of his full manhood; bringing a ripe scholarship, a mind naturally strong and thoroughly trained by the closest habits of application and study, a thorough knowledge of his profession, and an absolute devotion to the cause in which he was engaged, he filled the position to which he had been chosen with the greatest success and honor, continuously down to the time when he was summoned hence by the Master. In all these years, he was a leader in the church, as author, teacher, and preacher, ever ready to aid and strengthen her friends; and a formidable champion in her defence against the attacks of her foes, the founder of some of her most glorious enterprises, and the sharer of some of the greatest triumphs.

But it is chiefly to him as pastor of this church and congregation we would pay our tribute. This position he filled for a period of more than fourteen years, commencing in 1858; and those of us who sat under his ministry can bear loving testimony to the power, the progress, the influence, and prosperity of the church during that time. Truly the "Lord did guide him continually;" and this his church was "like a watered garden and spring of water, whose waters failed not." During this pastorate he was performing his duties as professor in the Seminary, and writing those books which will live after him and be an honor to his name, in guiding and assisting those in search of truth. His life was one of actual active service in the cause of the Master. His work will testify that he wrought with labor and travail night and day, neither an idler nor drone; setting an example to the rising ministry of earnest and abundant service. He was called away suddenly from the midst of his usefulness, and before age had compelled a relaxation from his labors. He continued to love and cherish his association with us until his sudden and lamented death. To us his Christian character was lovely; let his memory be blessed. At the time of his death, he had served more years as pastor, with one exception, than any others then living in our two cities; an aged and lamented one having preceded him into the presence of the Master only a few days, in a similar manner and almost as suddenly.

The lives and the deaths of these, who, with others, have gone to sit down with the patriarchs in the kingdom of God, are fraught with lessons to us. Let us remember the words of admonition of the lamented dead, in his last sermon to us: "The fathers, where are they? and the prophets, do they live for ever? But our work as a church is not yet done. The field remains, and widens as men pass by. Occupy it. God opens a path; but we must do the marching. His path is open only to those who go forward. One step at a time is all that God requires. Near by to Marah are the palm-trees and wells of Elim; and just by is the blessed country, and the clusters of Eshcol are there for such, and only such, as will go in and gather them."

To the stricken family we offer our sincere Christian sympathy and condolence in this the sad hour of their bereavement, and direct them to go for comfort to that source to which he, if living, would point them in all their troubles.

Resolutions of the Faculty of the United Presbyterian Theological Seminary at Allegheny.

Whereas, It has pleased God to remove by death Rev. M. W. JACOBUS, D.D., LL.D., Professor of Oriental and Biblical Literature in the Western Theological Seminary in this city, a position which he has occupied for twenty-five years, therefore, —

Resolved, 1. That we, the Faculty of the United Presbyterian Seminary at Allegheny, cherishing, as we have done, a high respect for this brother, not only as one who has, by his extensive erudition and indefatigable labors, advanced the cause of theological literature, but as one whose conduct has ever been that of the Christian gentleman, do hereby express the deep sorrow which his removal has awakened in our hearts, and our warm sympathy with those who have by this providence been deprived of his counsels, labors, and fellowship.

2. That, as a token of respect to the memory of the deceased, we will, as a Faculty, accompanied by the students of this Seminary, join in the procession that follows his remains from his dwelling in Allegheny to the First Presbyterian Church in Pittsburgh.

Resolutions of the Professors and Students of the Reformed Presbyterian Theological Seminary.

Whereas, We have heard with deep regret of the sudden death of Rev. Dr. MELANCTHON W. JACOBUS, Professor of Biblical Literature and Exegesis in the Western Theological Seminary of the Presbyterian Church: therefore, —

Resolved, 1. That we deeply sympathize with the family of Dr. JACOBUS in the loss of a beloved husband

and father, and earnestly pray that they may have the presence of the Comforter in this hour of their deep affliction.

2. That we sympathize with the Theological Seminary with which he was connected, in the loss of a professor so distinguished as a scholar and so esteemed for his Christian character and social qualities; and with the Presbyterian Church, with which he was so closely identified, not only as a professor in one of her most prominent seminaries, but as an earnest and efficient promoter of many of her most important schemes.

3. That in the death of Dr. JACOBUS we lament, in common with all the Evangelical churches, the loss of a sound and judicious commentator, whose labors have been abundantly blessed to many in assisting them to a more correct and satisfactory knowledge of the inspired Word of God.

4. That we recognize in this dispensation the hand of a merciful Providence. This good soldier of Christ died with his armor on. He was graciously spared much of the bitterness of death. He has been removed from a wide sphere of active usefulness here to a higher and wider sphere there where His servants serve Him. With loins girded and lamps burning, he heard the voice of the Bridegroom, and was ready. "Blessed are the dead who die in the Lord. They rest from their labors, and their works do follow them."

Resolutions of the Evangelical Ministerial Association of Pittsburgh.

As a ministerial association, united in a common faith, sharing the privileges of a covenant relationship in Christ our Lord, and engaged in a special and sacred calling, we feel the ties of our brotherhood to be the very bonds of peace, and our communion on earth the earnest of that which the saints in light enjoy for ever; for our fellowship is now with the Father, and with the Son, and with the Holy Spirit.

It has pleased our heavenly Father, whose we are, and whom we serve, — whose providence is always wise, however mysterious or afflicting to His children, — to remove from us, suddenly, our esteemed and beloved brother, the Rev. MELANCTHON W. JACOBUS, D.D., LL.D., a sincere believer in Jesus Christ, an able minister of the gospel, and a profound and successful educator in the things of the Spirit.

To-day we miss our brother's familiar form and face and voice; we suffer because our loss is great and irreparable; we sorrow because we are personally bereaved. We wonder why one so dear, so near, so genial, so true, so strong, — why one so ready, competent, and willing to help us by his counsel, and share with us in toil and sacrifice,

— should be thus unexpectedly removed from our ranks. And yet we know that for such to die is gain, that our missing brother's life is "hid with Christ in God," and that there shall be reunion and reassociation of all believers by and by.

We shall strive to emulate the worthy example of our absent friend and brother by a more consecrated service, by renewed diligence and zeal, by patience, vigilance, courage, charity, and faith like his; and, like him, we shall try to live in such constant communion with our Saviour as to be ready, at any moment, to depart, and be "for ever with the Lord."

We tender our heartfelt sympathies to the bereaved family of our dear brother JACOBUS, and commend them to the gracious protection of One who abideth with them always, even to the end of the world.

To the students of the Western Theological Seminary, bereft of a teacher both revered and loved, we extend the warm hand-pressure of a silent grief which words may not express.

With family, fellow-professors, and students, with the church of his early and eventful life, with the Christian community at large, with the great multitude of those who have been edified and comforted by his books, so widely circulated both in our own and foreign lands, we mingle our tears to-day; and yet with all do we rejoice in the hope of immortality and eternal life. "Then shall the redeemed of the Lord return and come with singing to Zion; and everlasting joy shall be upon their head; they shall obtain joy and gladness, and sorrow and sighing shall flee away."

Resolutions of the Baptist Ministers of Pittsburgh and Allegheny.

Whereas, It has been brought to the knowledge of the Conference of Baptist Ministers of Pittsburgh and Allegheny that the Rev. Professor M. W. JACOBUS, D.D., departed this life on Saturday morning last:

Resolved, That we unitedly express our sympathy with the sorrowing relations; our esteem for him as a Christian brother and as a divine; and that Rev. R. W. Pearson, D.D., Rev. J. S. Wrightnour, and Rev. Wm. H. McKinney be appointed to attend his funeral on behalf of this Conference.

Resolutions of the Cliosophic Society of the College of New Jersey.

Whereas, God in His own wise providence has called to himself our fellow-member, Rev. Dr. M. W. JACOBUS, of the class of '34; and *whereas*, in his death, the Cliosophic Society mourns the loss of an honored and worthy friend, whose high Christian character, intellectual worth, and devotion to her interests have won for him a name which we all love to recall: therefore, be it—

Resolved, That, whilst our hearts are saddened at the thought that we shall see his face and hear his voice no more, yet we reverently bow in submission to God's will; knowing that He who doth lead us into darkness will bring us again to the light.

Resolved, That, in this dark shadow of affliction, we would tender our deepest sympathy and condolence to the bereaved family. To them there is left a father's memory and a father's prayers; to us, an example of a higher Christian life.

Resolved, That, in token of our regard, the hall be draped for thirty days, and a committee be appointed to attend his funeral.

Letter from Great Britain.

The sudden death of the distinguished Dr. Jacobus has caused wide-spread sorrow here as well as with you. It was meet and fitting that Drs. Hall and McCosh should join in the sad obsequies to represent the churches here on the mournful occasion. The distinguished doctor belonged to the entire Catholic church. His learning, his works, his name, and his fame are its common heritage, pregnant with enduring preciousness, rich with undying, noble inspiration. Presbyterianism may claim them with special joy, but cannot monopolize them as exclusively its possessions. The eulogies pronounced over him were appreciatory and just, free from extravagant adulation. In chastened, correct, and discriminating language all the panegyrics were embodied.

The following extract from a sermon by Dr. Jacobus may fitly conclude this memorial volume : —

For to me *to live* is CHRIST, — Christ for the *rule* of living, Christ for the *motive* of living, Christ for the *ideal* of living, Christ for the *source* and *spring* of living, Christ for the very *definition* of living. Then, indeed, you may afford to be in a happy balance between two worlds, — to have Christ *with* you *on earth*, or *to be with* Christ in *heaven*. Walking *with God*, like Enoch, it cannot be but that you shall go up to God *virtually without death*, without its *sting* and *curse* and *bitterness*.

And when, some day, men will inquire why your place is vacant in the business circle, in the household, and in the sanctuary, it will be said, " He walked with God, and *was not*, for God took him." He went up, not in any chariot of fire, but on the soft wing of the covenant angel. From where he daily climbed to the topmost round of Jacob's ladder, he stepped *directly* into heaven. From where he trod on the high road of Christian living, far up towards the celestial city, he found the door *wide open* into the golden streets of the New Jerusalem.

Cambridge: Press of John Wilson & Son.

Printed in Dunstable, United Kingdom